facades
architectural details

Imprint
The Deutsche Bibliothek is registering
this publication in the Deutsche
Nationalbibliographie; detailed
bibliographical information can be found
on the internet at http://dnb.ddb.de

ISBN 978-3-938780-38-1 (Hardcover)
ISBN 978-3-938780-43-5 (Softcover)

© 2008 by Verlagshaus Braun
www.verlagshaus-braun.de

1st edition 2008

Editor:
Markus Sebastian Braun
Editorial staff:
Susanne Laßwitz
Translation:
Alice Bayandin, María José Garibotto
Graphic concept and layout:
Michaela Prinz
Reproduction:
LVD Gesellschaft für Datenverarbeitung
mbH, Berlin

facades

architectural details

BRAUN

contents

brussels, rue du progrès

façades – more than a mask

The word "façade" is derived from the Latin "facies" or Italian "faccia" for "face". The façade is therefore the "face of the house". Seeing as the Italian Renaissance (to no small extent) shaped building theory and conceptuality throughout Europe with its complex house and façade designs, the term "facciate" to describe a façade in the sense of the outer side or front of a building stands it in good stead. In the 16th century it drifted to the then leading architectural sphere in France, whereupon it took on its French form "façade" as is used today in English.

The *Lexikon der Kunst* (*Encyclopedia of Art*; Leipzig, 1989, Volume 2) describes façades: "In the most general sense, the word façade refers to any outer side, in particular, the front of a building. It is usually the side with the main entrance, so usually the one onto a (public) square or street, which can, in turn, both be influenced considerably by façades. … Depending on the pretence and function, a main façade can be differentiated from a side façade; a street from an inner courtyard or garden façade, especially in castle structures. As a result, the existing architectonic system of wall paneling can be integrated with different degrees of magnitude. Unlike the above description of the term, a stronger viewpoint removes the phrase "façade" further from the visual side, seeing in the latter the projected geometric view of the side of a building construction, in the former, however, a freestanding or partially freestanding building construction in front of the actual building, which does not have to portray the interior in any way". Following its own rules, this autonomy of the façade forms the basis of the figurative sense of the word.

Depending on the construction style and the building, there are countless elements of façade design in existence; from pylons, pillared halls and portico façades in antiquity, depicting scenes on church buildings, tower and portal façades in the Middle Ages to gable façades, figurine niches, and oriels / corner towers later. While the beginning saw mostly ecclesiastical architecture and manor buildings feature complex façades, this architecture started becoming more common on town halls, armories, middle-class houses, and theaters in earlier modern times. Even more representative than the front door of a house was a complex façade, which portrayed the power and social status of the occupant. Mosaics, paintings, figures, and scenes all contributed to making the façade more colorful and livelier, and often represented a piece of artwork in itself. This often superseded the function of the house, as is mentioned in the same article: "While these independent façades most undeniably gave the building, in older examples, its own sense of grandeur, later versions often contained rather modest complexes behind grandiose façades. In the 19th century, it was often the case that elegant inner courtyards hid behind the ostentatious historical façades of city streets. Here, the function of the façade was to make the homes behind them appear luxurious, which influenced the amount of rent charged". Finally, the façade dissociated itself from what hid behind it, from the so-called "curtain façade", and ceased to have a static-constructive function anymore.

Earlier epochs seem to have reserved the façade as a sign of respectable representative buildings. The article "façade" in the *Oekonomische Encyclopaedie (Economic Encyclopedia)* by Johann Georg Krünitz (published 1773) says: "Façade", the entire front wall of a respectable building for gazing upon from either the street side or from an inner yard or garden. The term façade is not used for the front of common houses, rather "la face de la maison". A façade with very few decorations around the doors and window is termed simple, from the French, "façade simple". On the other hand, one designed according to the rules of a certain order of columns, with bas-relief on the plinths (plinthes), on the entablature (corniches), and other ledges, sometimes also with etched or carved trophies, with busts, statues, etc. are termed richly decorated, or in French, "façade riche". Sometimes "façade" can be understood as only the front elevation or orthographic outline of a façade. In a more limited sense, it can mean just the front or front gable of a large house".

In contrast, *Meyer's Conversations-Lexikon (Meyer's Conversation Lexicon)* from 1887 (Leipzig, 4th Edition, Volume 6) deals with the variety of façade designs and calls a façade "the architecturally designed outer side, or in a simpler sense, the front of a building. The architectural design of a façade is dependent on the room arrangement on the interior and should show this on the outside of the building as best possible." In this way, the different floors should be marked with "continuous cornicing", which "prevent emptiness and uniformity on an even outer wall". The design of the interior should also "express itself in the façade and its design, e.g. by coupling multiple windows from the same room or separating them from one another with broad wall spaces or wall pillar positioning". In order to establish a coherent overall impression, the correct positioning of the door also has to be taken into account: "A door, an entrance of a façade can add life and interest and from an aesthetic or artistic point of view, it should be seen as a flaw if the door is positioned at the side or back of the house. A well-positioned door can make the façade appear inviting and friendly. While, at the same time, a more richly designed door, for example, raised up a few steps, with or without pillars or columns, with a well designed lintel or an especially, flat gable adds diversity and dignity to a façade. With annexes, projecting balconies or oriels, the façade can be especially enriched". Clear and proportional design of the individual elements is essential; it should be aspired towards to "dissect larger wall areas using wall pillars or niches with statues, columns or half columns; caryatids or atlases as carriers of the entablatures, arabesque ornaments under door and window roofing, open work on balconies, and arabesque and ornamental friezes, etc.; occasional application of painting with long-lasting, non-garish colors, which would detract from the profiles of the cornice, door, and window decoration". To finish, the lexicon entry from 1887 notes that: "In recent times façade painting, following on from the passion the Italian and German Renaissance showed for color, has achieved wider popularity. Entire façades of Sgraffito painting in black, brown, red, yellow, etc. are covered with glass mosaics and polychrome paintings. These different techniques are also combined".

"Sgraffito" painting is known to us nowadays in a form, which tends to annoy many house owners: as "graffiti", which make an unwanted appearance usually under cover of darkness on the façades of houses and public buildings. The French philosopher Jean Baudrillard saw in these wild spray-can creations a "revolution of symbols" as a sign of modernity. The wild, unruly appearance of such symbols, pictures and logos, whose sense is more often than not undecipherable, a type of public secret language. For him, graffiti is an example of "speaking without responding" with symbolic codes, which become detached from any kind of meaning and purely serve their own unknown purpose. The transition from art to "mere scribbling" is fluent and is, as many things, in the eye of the beholder.

There is one fundamental element of façade design, which leads on to the figurative meaning of façade: façade painting. It was most prevalent in the Italian Renaissance in the form of fresco-secco painting and "mostly serves to emphasize picture and space illusions by affecting the perspective. This is also known as "tromp d'oeil". The blossoming period of façade painting stretches from the early Renaissance to the end of the Baroque period. To a certain extent, it achieved illusions which partially or totally swamp out the façade structure." As mentioned in the article "façade painting" in the aforementioned Encyclopedia of Art, it aimed either at portraying edifying, historical, or mythological scenes,

a type of "public paintings gallery" or "home cinema", or the creation of amazing spatial illusions, which expanded non-existent depth dimensions.

It is precisely here where the figurative meaning of the façade is found, which rather means something like a "mask, dressing, or illusion". "That is just a façade" means, plain-talking, that it is all just a pretty appearance, an optical illusion, which in reality does not represent anything other than a skewed perception. The viewer is made a fool of, led up the garden path, tricked, and possibly disappointed. Straight away, the term that has since become common-day occurs to us all: the Potemkin Villages. The apparent story behind it is well-known: In 1783, Prince Grigori Aleksandrovich Potemkin (1739-1791), former favorite, advisor, and bedfellow ("Tsar of the Night") of the Russian tsarina Catherine II the Great, was handed the task of colonizing the southern Russian areas with a number of cities. While checking progress, he showed the tsarina a number of housing backdrops or façades from a safe distance on a boat, which greatly pleased the tsarina. Nowadays, the Potemkin Villages are historically a nasty slander of the brave work the constructional pioneers did in creating something rather amazing, but the term and the story are too good to be forgotten. The advice remains, however, that one should be wary of mere illusion and pure façades, i.e. the many existing Potemkin Villages out there.

Markus Hattstein

amsterdam

amsterdam, spuistraat 303

rietlandpark 353 | borneolaan

amsterdam, prins hendrikkade 600

amsterdam, rietlandpark 353

nieuwezijds voorburgwal 35-39 | beursplein

above left, above mid, below left, below mid, right: amsterdam. oosterdokskade 143 (openbare bibliotheek) |
strawinskylaan 1 | oosterdokskade | oostelijke handelskade | baron g.a. tindalplein 2 (the whale)

athens

athens, kaningos 21

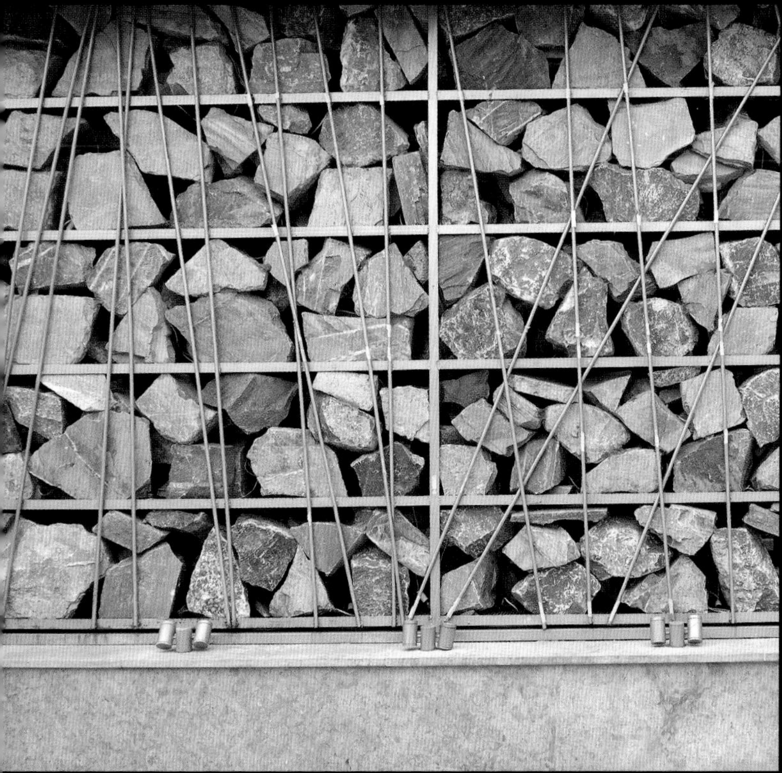

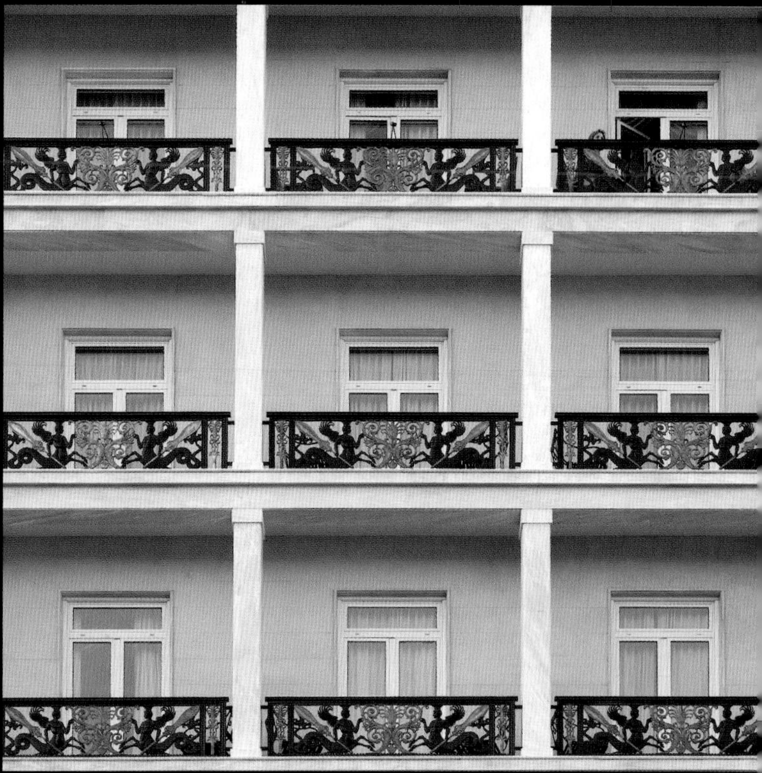

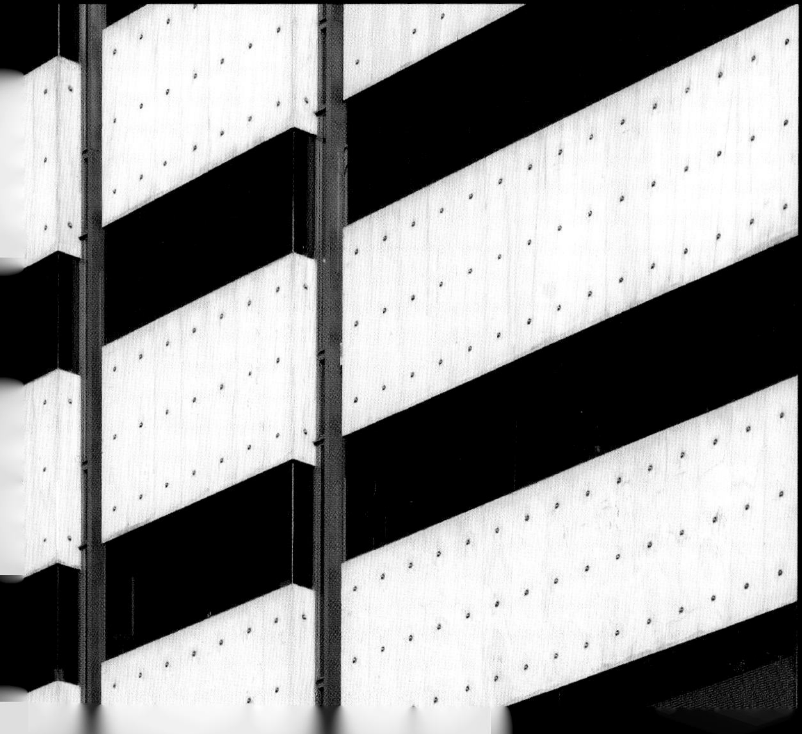

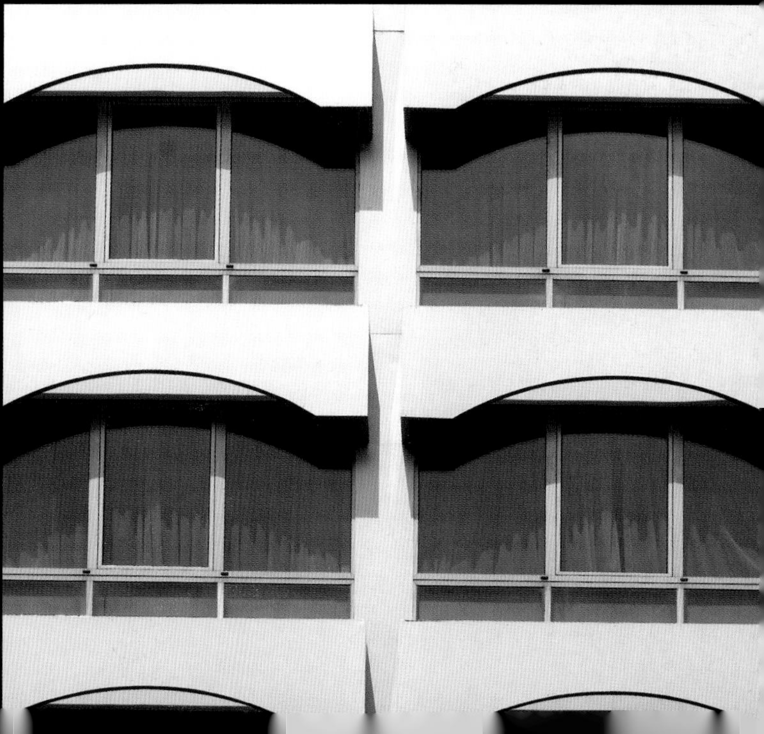

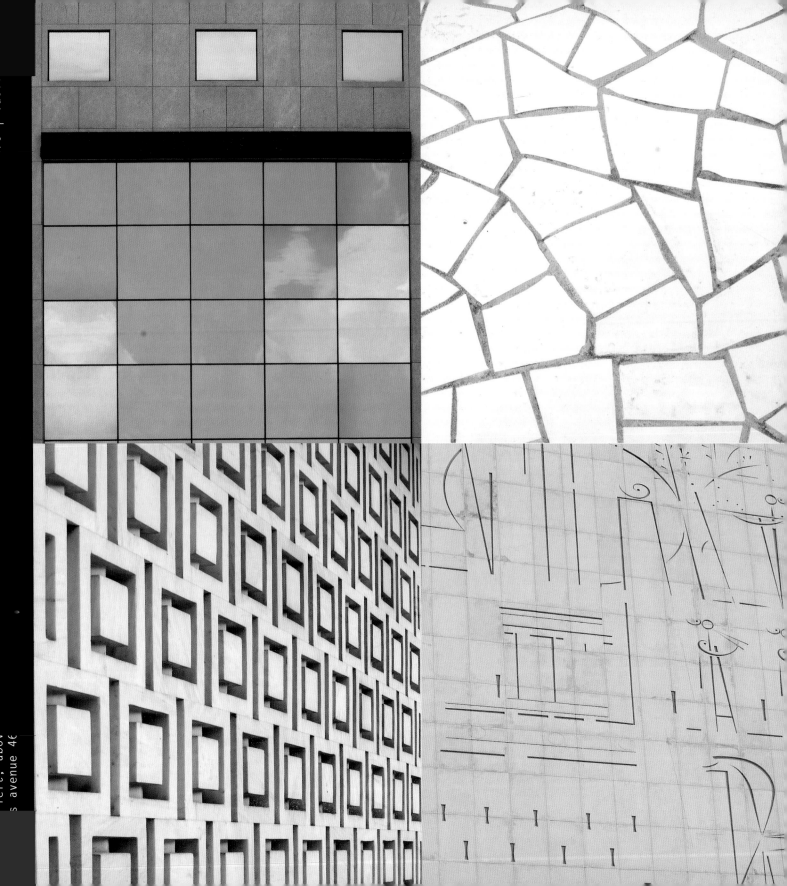

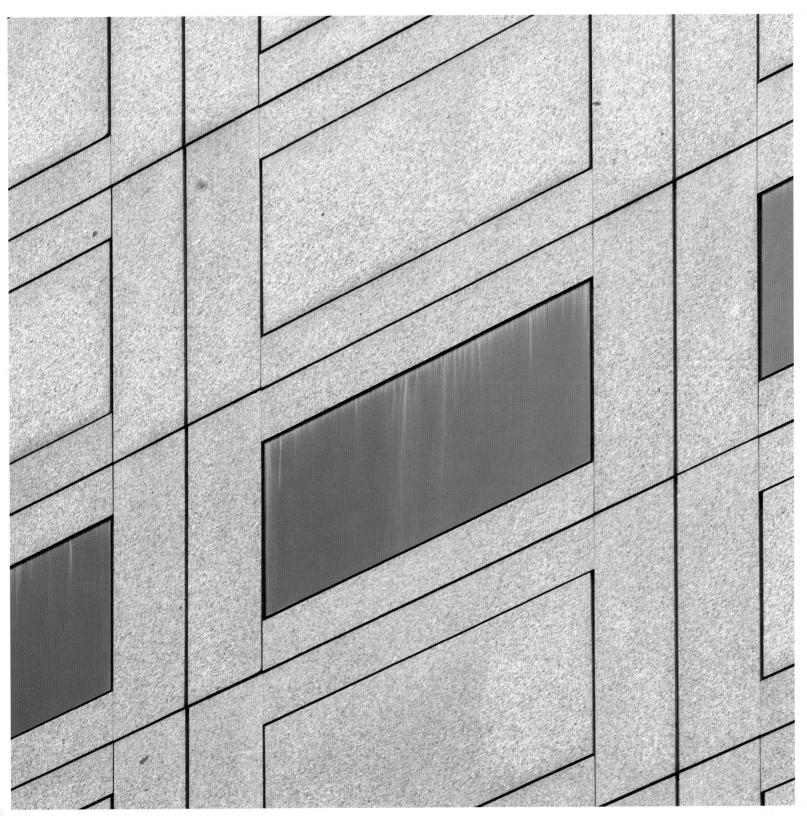

athens, akadimias 68

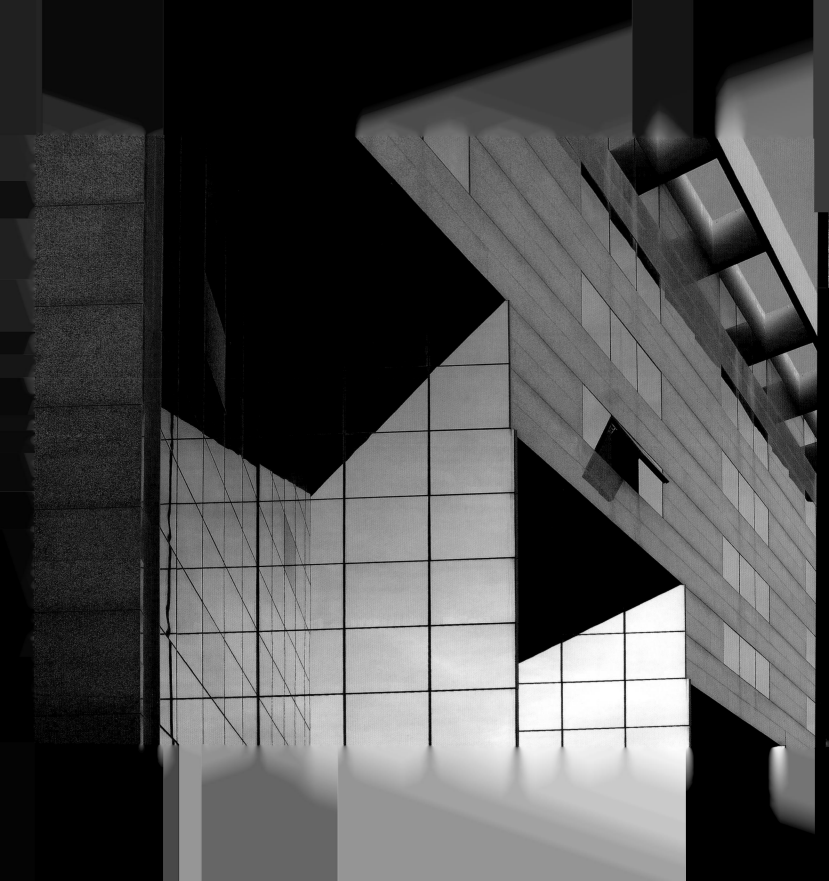

korai 1

barcelona

barcelona, passeig de gràcia 43 (casa batlló)

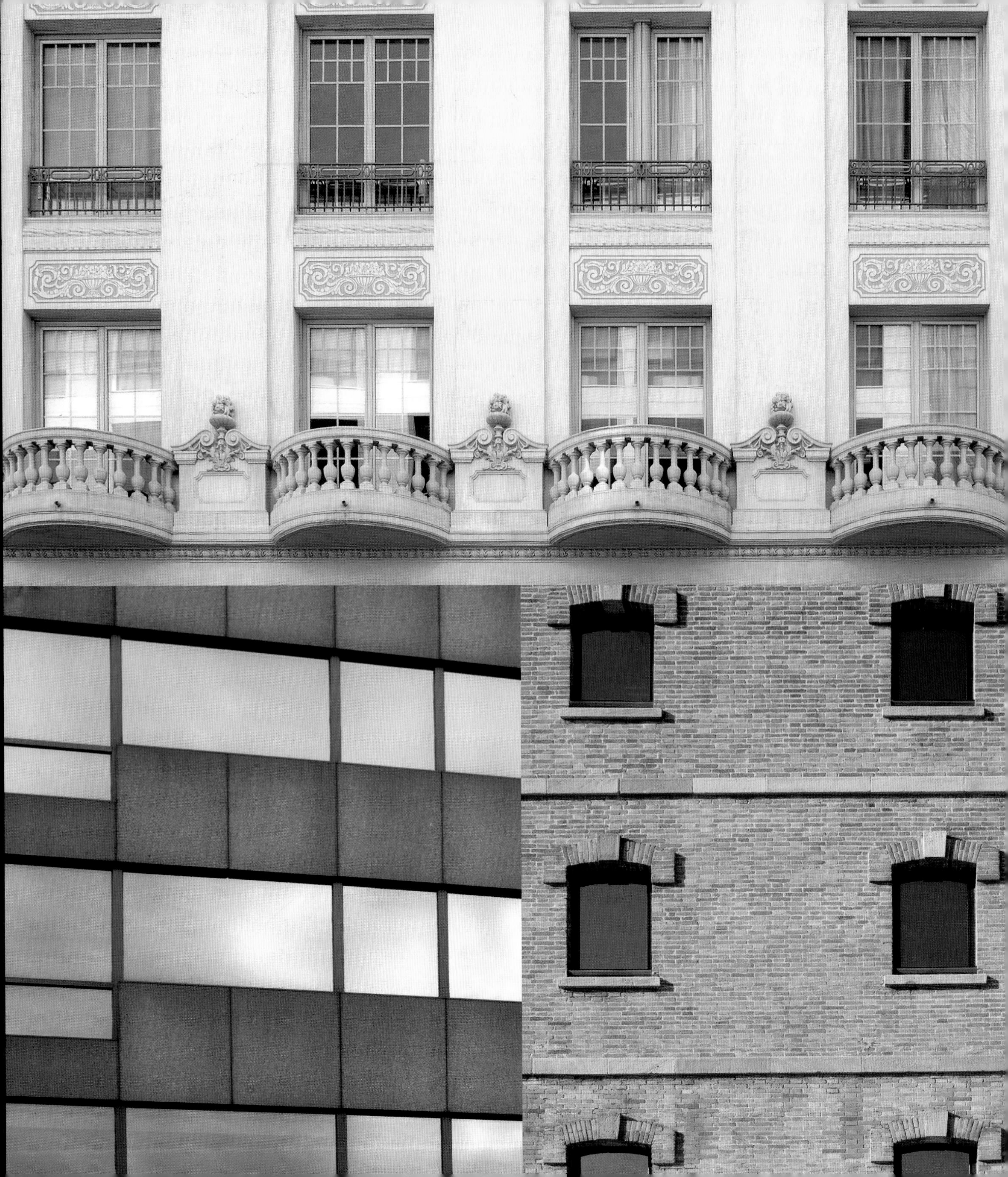

palacio del mar (museo de historia de cataluña)

barcelona, marina 19-21

avinguda marquès de comillas 13 (poble español de montjuïc) | moll d'espanya, 5-2 planta (maremagnum) | paseo
de gràcia 92 (casa mila / la pedrera)

comillas (pavelló de mies van der rohe) | via laietana 20 | moll d'espanya, 5-2 planta (maremagnum)

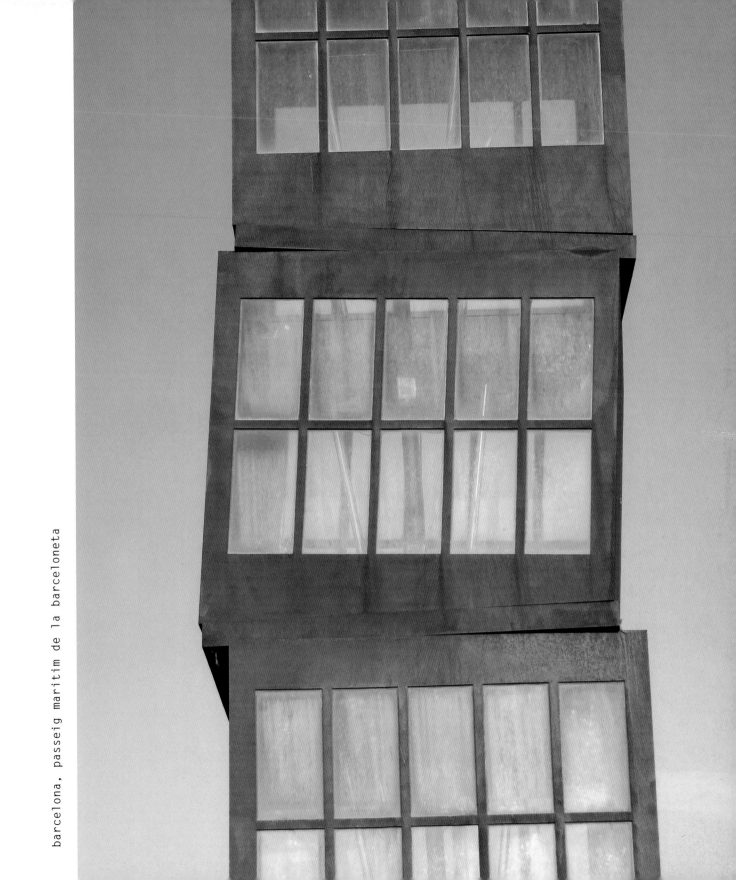

barcelona, passeig maritim de la barceloneta

berlin

berlin, alt-moabit 143-145 (polizei- und feuerwache)

above left, above right, below left, below right: berlin, klingelhöferstraße 18 (sap gebäude) | klingelhöferstraße 3

(mexikanische botschaft) | rauchstraße 1 (nordische botschaften) | hiroshimastraße 12-16 (landesvertretung nrw)

left, above right, below right: berlin, klingelhöferstraße | reichpietschufer 60 (gasag verwaltungsgebäude) | karl-marx-allee 33 (kino international)

berlin, lindenstraße 9-14 (jüdisches museum)

berlin, invalidenstraße 50-51 (hamburger bahnhof - museum für gegenwart)

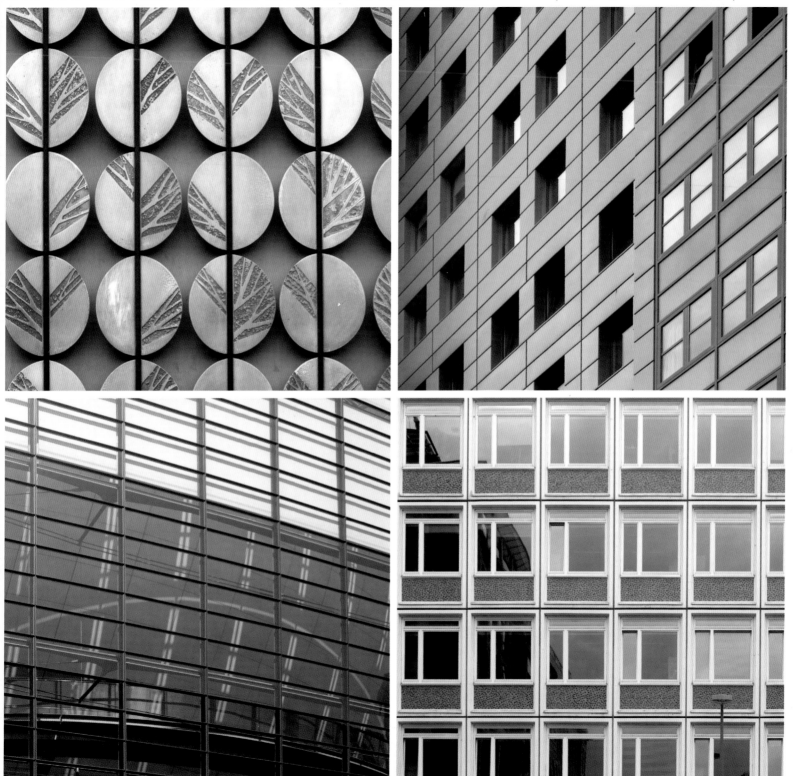

potsdamer platz | behrenstraße 40-41 (studentenwerk berlin)

brussels

brussels, quartier léopold

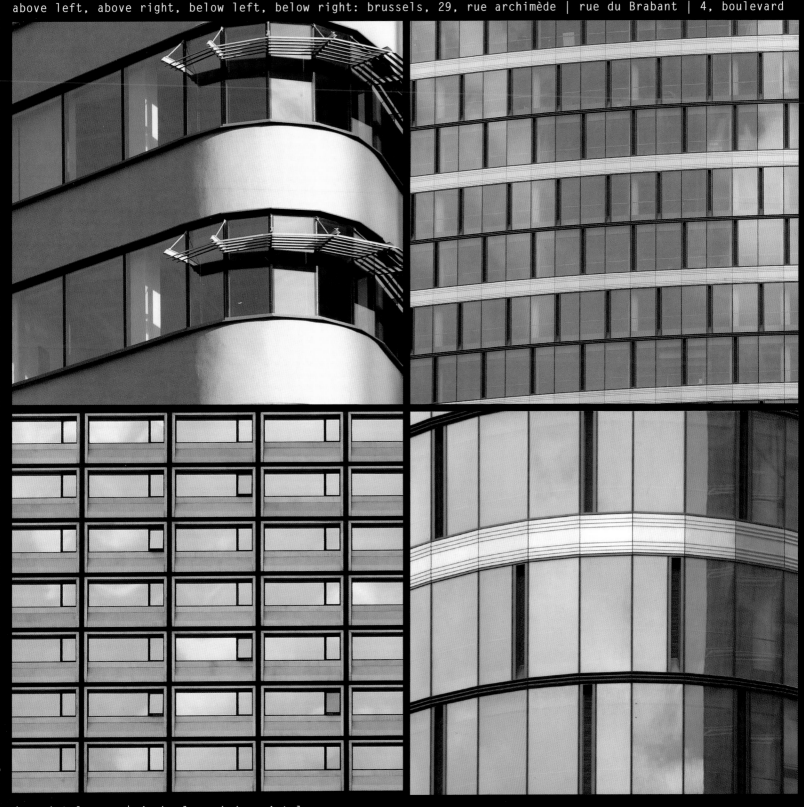

above left, above right, below left, below right: brussels, 200, rue de la loi | 38, chaussée de wavre | rue de la loi | rue wiertz

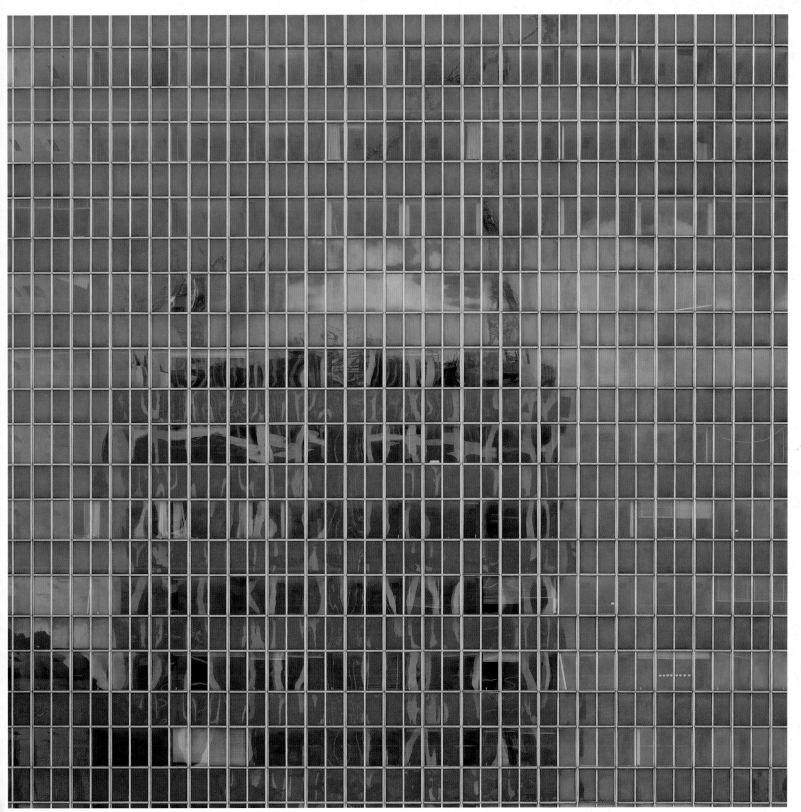

brussels, 204, rue royale (cité administrative de l'etat)

brussels, rue du progrès

9, chaussée d'anvers | 1, rue de boiteaux

above left, above right, below left, below right: brussels, sinter-goedeleplein | 29, rue vautier | 29, rue vautier | 29, rue vautier | grand place

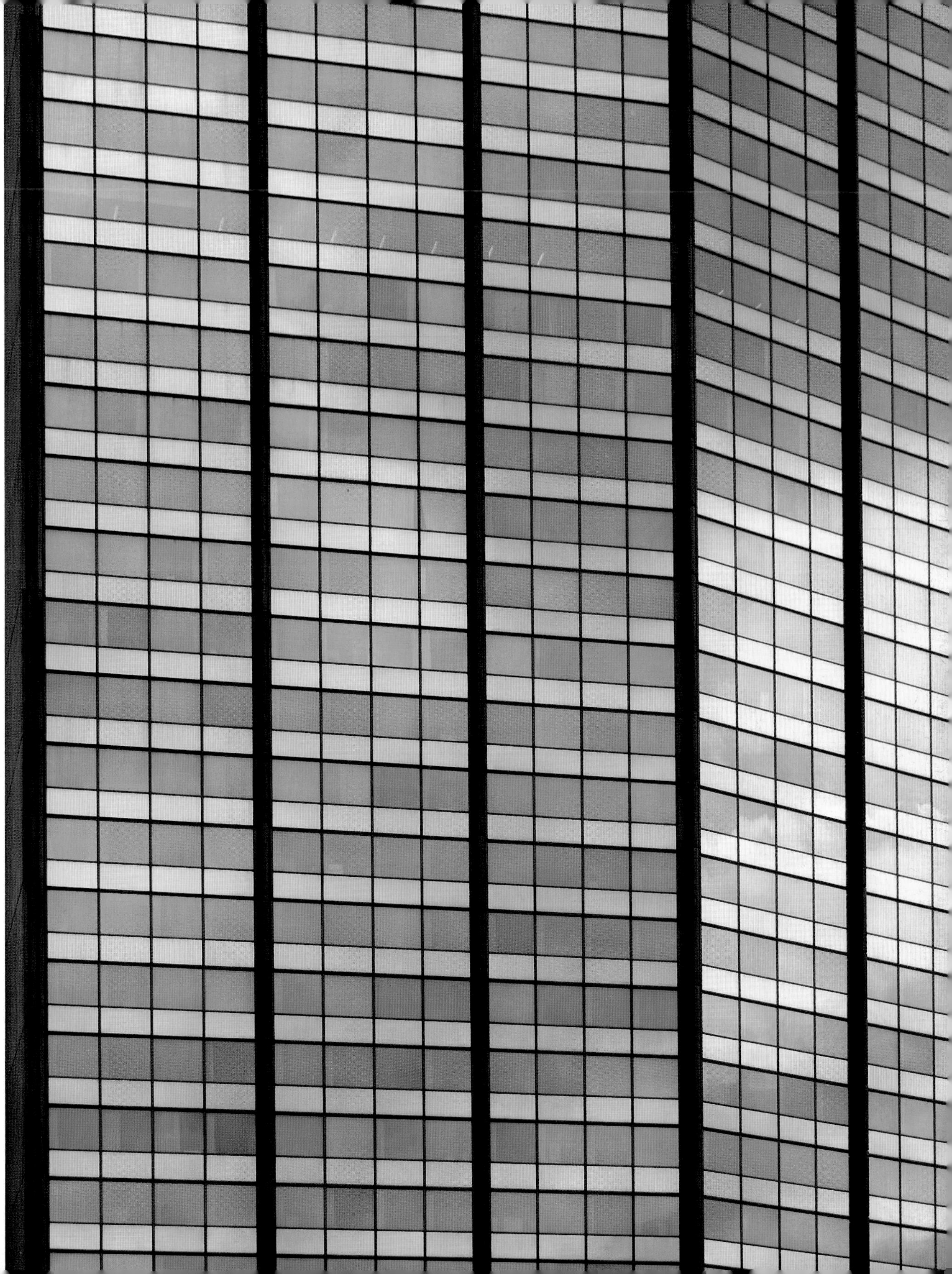

brussels, rue de bériot

budapest

budapest, dózsa györgy utca 84b

budapest, csaba utca 5

budapest, nyugati tér

above left, above right, below: budapest, millenáris park | deák ferenc utca 12 |

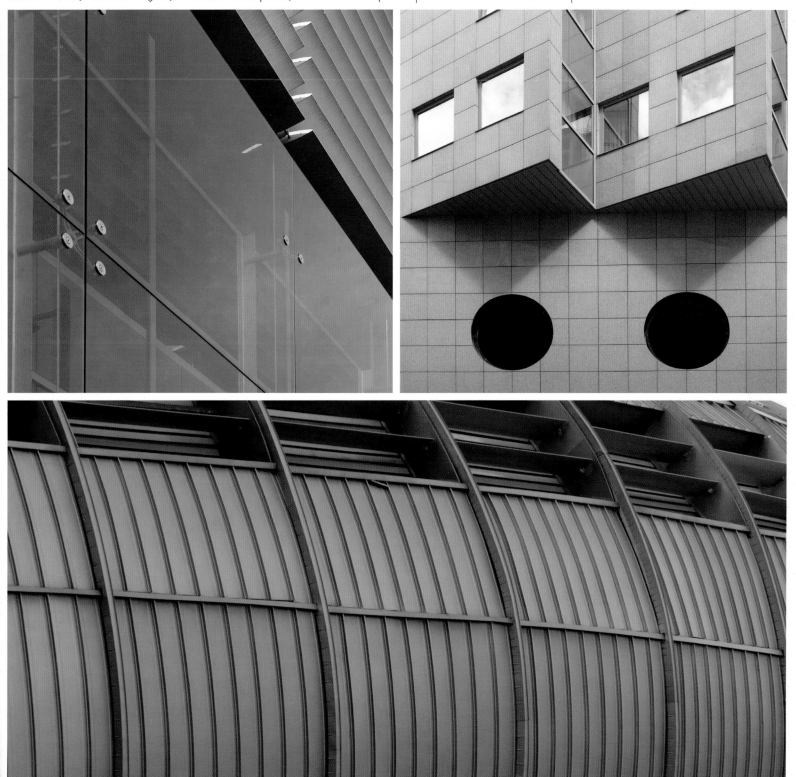

stefánia utca 2 (papp lászló sportaréna)

színház) | hess andras ter 1-3 (hilton hotel) | dózsa györgy utca 37 (mcsarnok)

budapest, deák ferenc utca 17

copenhagen, radhuspladsen 57 (palace hotel)

above left, above right, below left, below right: copenhagen, bernstorffsgade 31 | grønnegade 2 | bernstorffgade 31 | h.c. andersen boulevard 27

copenhagen, strandgade 27 a

cracow

ulica grodzka

above left, above right, below left, below right: cracow, ulica powiśle 12 | aleja mickiewicza 30 | aleja krasińskiego 18 | ulica sienna

cracow, aleja krasińskiego 1

helsinki

helsinki, aleksanterinkatu

above left, above right, below left, below right: helsinki, mannerheimaukio | mannerheimaukio | mannerheimintie | mannerheimintie

helsinki, mannerheimaukio

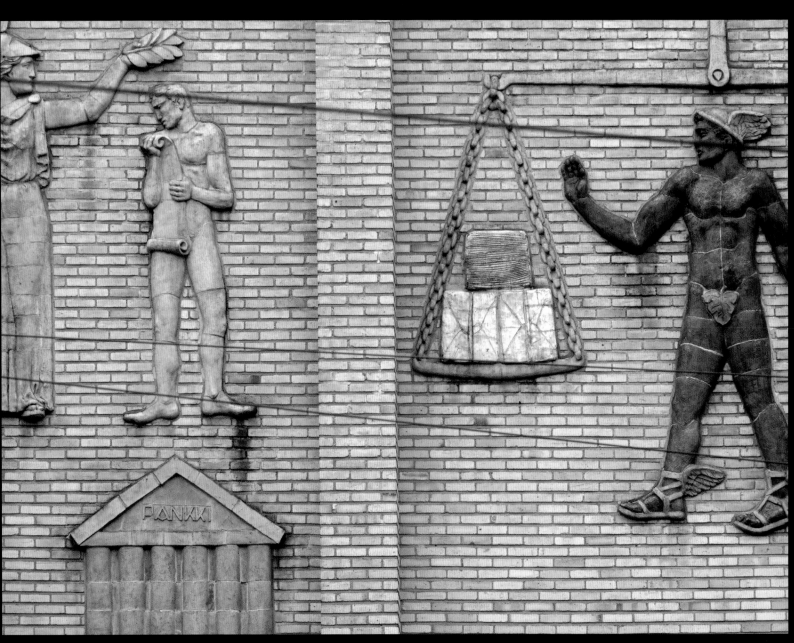

helsinki, runeberginkatu 14 (helsinki school of economics)

istanbul

istanbul, prof. kazim ismail gürkan caddesi

istiklal caddesi | çırağan caddesi 32 (çırağan palace kempinski) | istikla caddesi

istanbul, kemankes caddesi

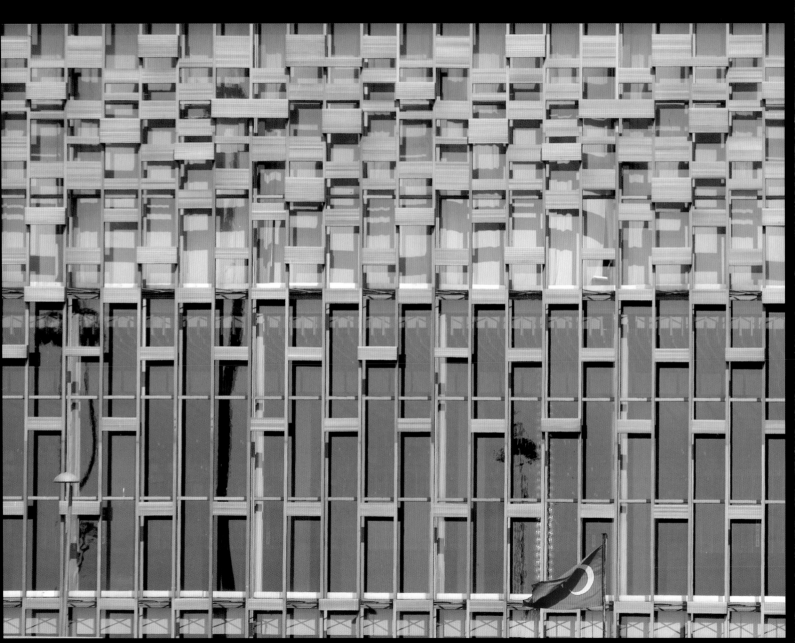

istanbul, taksim meydan

(dolmabahçe sarayi) | taksim meydan

lisbon, azulejos

nações (parque expo 98) | avenida antónio augusto de aguiar 68 | parque das nações (parque expo 98)

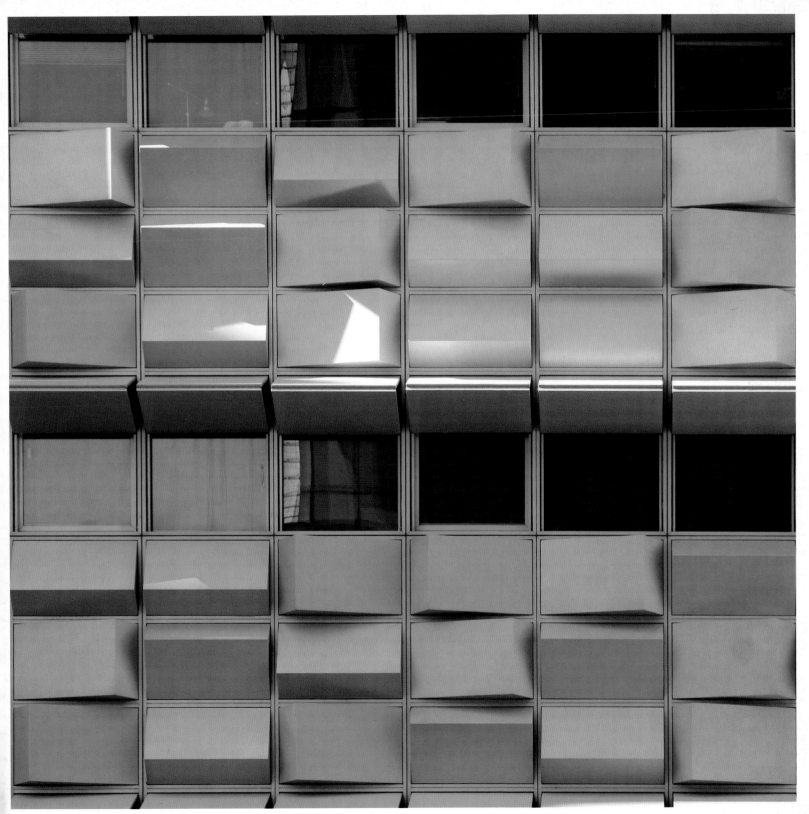

lisbon, parque das nações (parque expo 98)

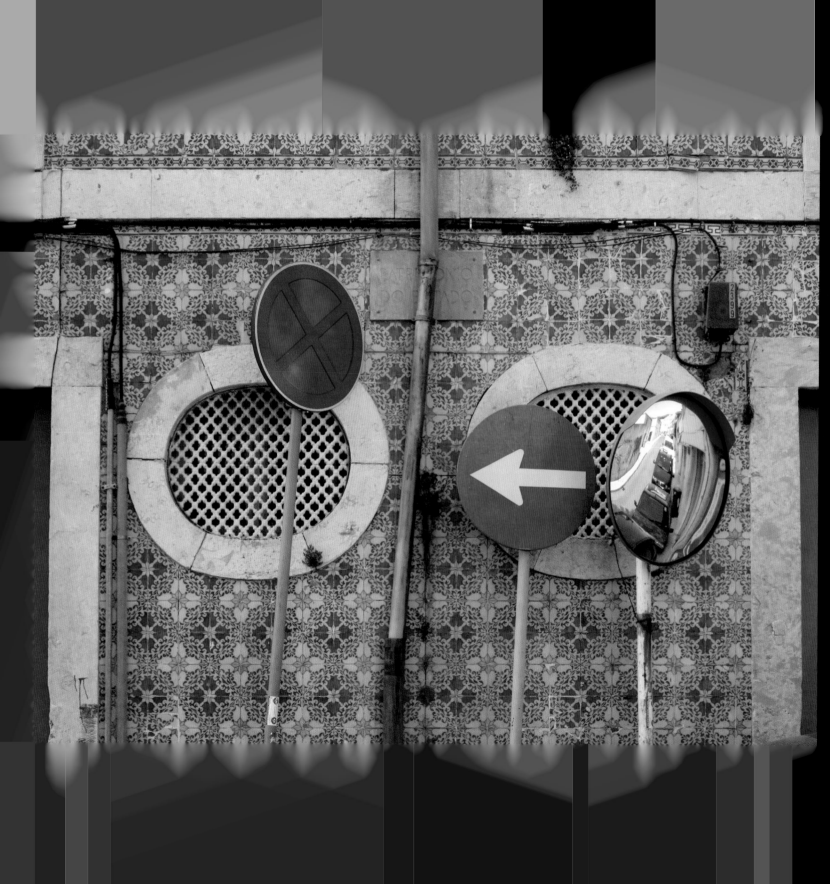

above left, above mid, below left, below mid, right: lisbon, parque das nações (parque expo 98) | parque das nações (parque expo 98) | parque das nações (parque expo 98) | parque das nações (parque expo 98) | parque das nações (parque expo 98)

ljubljana, miklošičeva cesta 8 (zadružne gospodarske banke)

trg republike

above left, above right, below left, below right: ljubljana, dalmatinova ulica | trg republike | tabor 4 | karunova ulica 14a

ljubljana, dalmatinova ulica 2

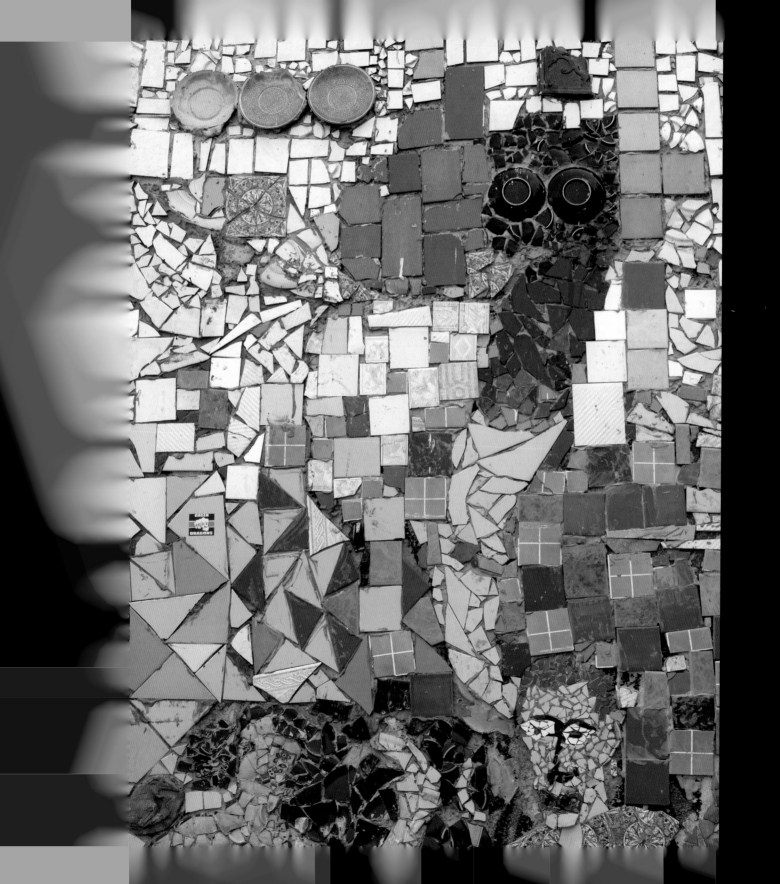

kapitarjeva ulica 2

london

london, parliament street (houses of parliament)

above left, above right, below left, below right: london, 79-81 euston road (st pancras) | cromwell road

(natural history museum) | 161 piccadilly | 55 kensington high street

above left, above right, below left, below right: london, 1 coleman street | 123 victoria street (ashdown house) | 123 victoria street (ashdown house) | 55 victoria street

london, 20 bury street (swiss re building)

london, 11 gainsford street (butler's wharf)

st georges wharf (shad thames)

above left, above right, below left, below right: london, 22 hertsmere road | one canada square | 64-68 exhibition road (the church of jesus christ of latter-day saints) | south kensington campus (imperial college)

london, 101-111 kensington high street (barkers arcade)

paris

paris, cour napoléon (louvre)

above left, above right, below left, below right: paris, 193 rue de bercy | esplanade de la défense |
esplanade de la défense | 1 rue des fossés saint-bernard (institut du monde arabe)

above left, above right, below left, below right: paris, esplanade de la défense |
1 rue paul klee | 1 rue edmont flamand

paris, esplanade de la défense / parvis de la défense

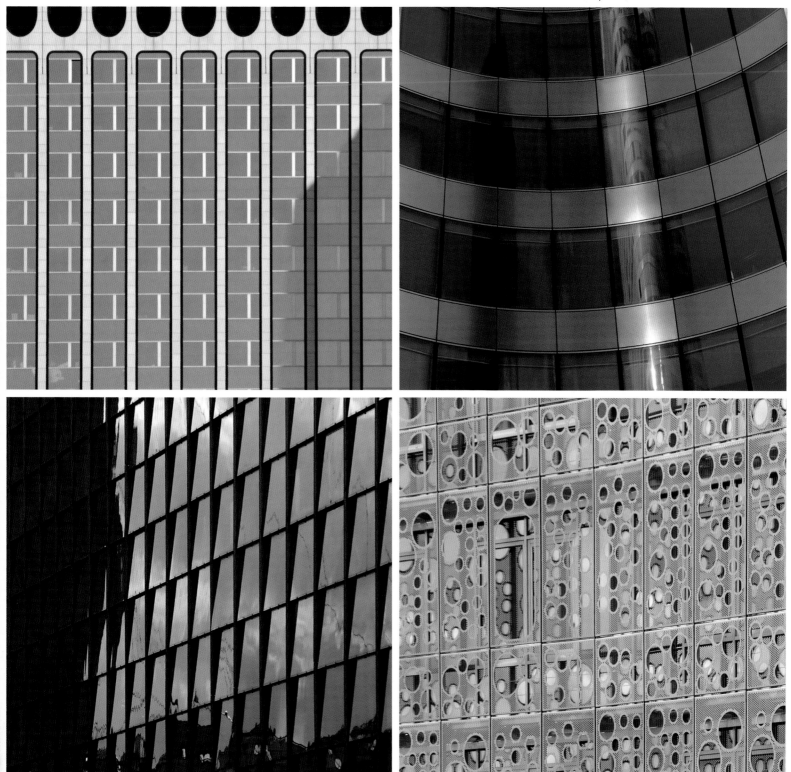

(tour edf) | place de la coupole (tour fiat) | 4 place jussien (faculté des sciences)

above left, above mid, below left, below mid, right: paris, place georges pompidou (centre pompidou) | pont charles de gaulle / quai austerlitz | quai de la gare | esplanade de la défense | 41-47 quai austerlitz

prague, koulova 15 (hotel crowne plaza)

náměstí curieovych 100 (president hotel) | staré proboštství | nový svet 5

above left, above right, below left, below right: prague, na příkopě 1 | kotva 7 | vinohradska 10 | na příkopě 19

prague, wilsonova 2

ovocný trh 10 | škrétova 12

riga

riga, škūņu ielā

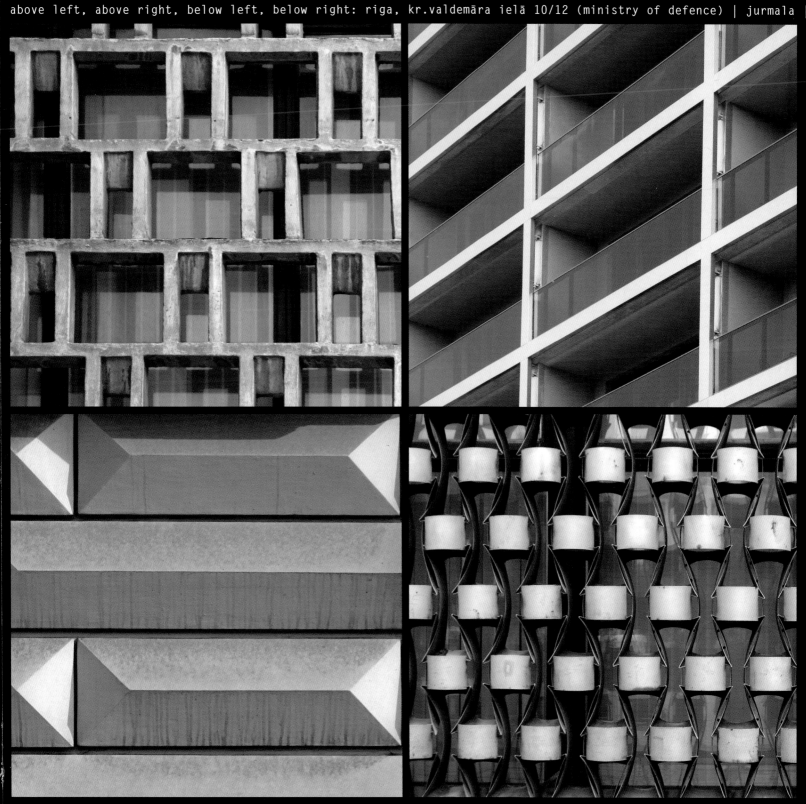

above left, above right, below left, below right: riga, kr.valdemāra ielā 10/12 (ministry of defence) | jurmala

strelnieku laukums 1 (museum of the occupation of latvia) | elisabetes ielā

above left, above right, below left, below right: riga, azenes ielā | kalpaka bulvāris | krišjāņa valdemāra ielā | reimersa ielā 1 (reval hotel ridzene)

riga, krišjāņa valdemāra ielā

riga, ieriķu ielā 3 (tirdzniecības centrs)

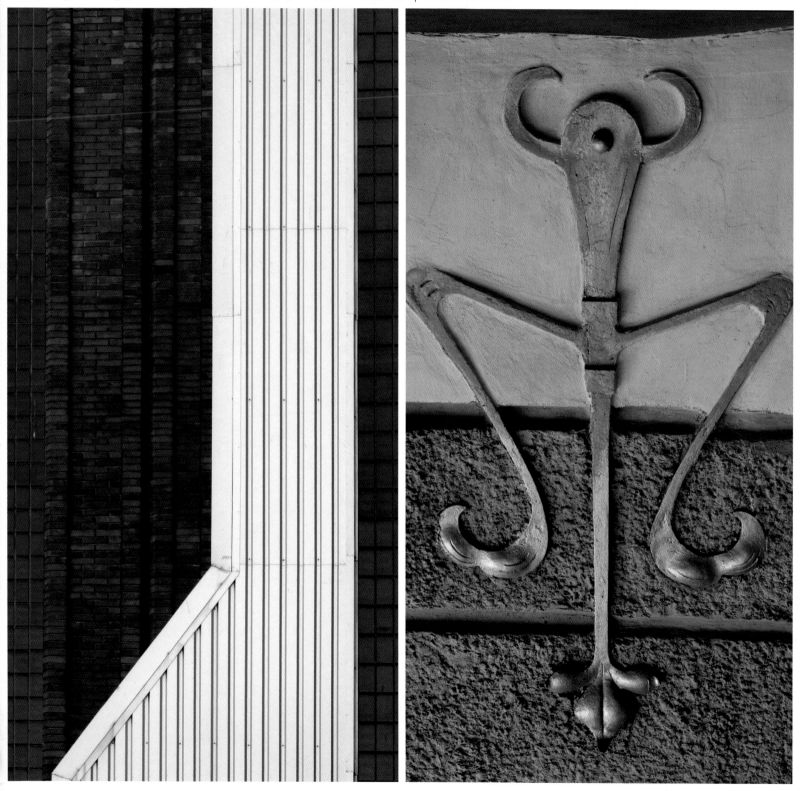

rome, viale della civiltà del lavoro

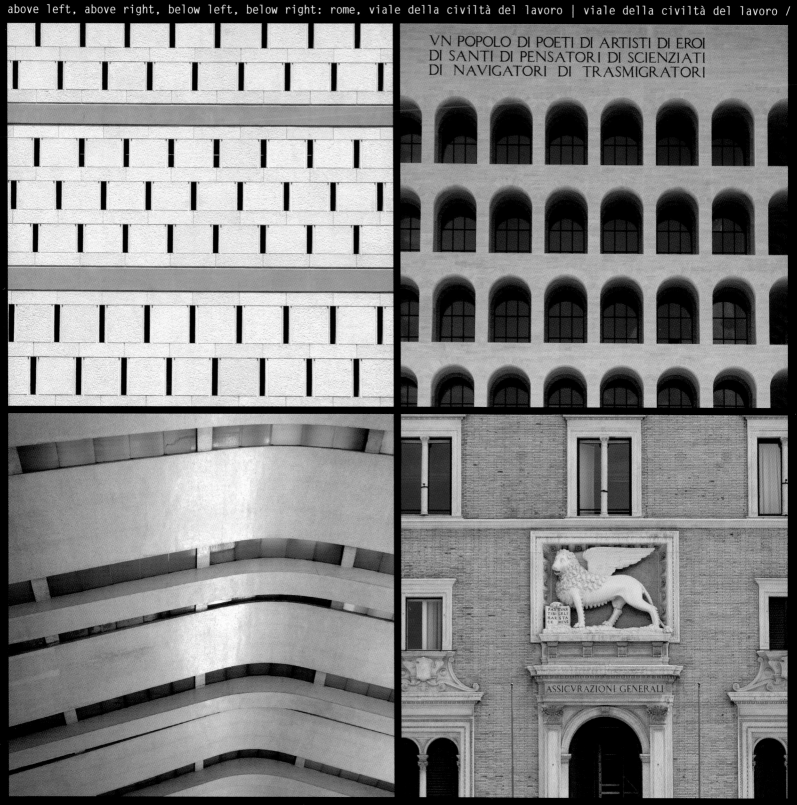

VN POPOLO DI POETI DI ARTISTI DI EROI
DI SANTI DI PENSATORI DI SCIENZIATI
DI NAVIGATORI DI TRASMIGRATORI

ASSICVRAZIONI GENERALI

(palazzo della civiltà del lavoro) | piazza die cinquecento (stazione termini - giovanni paolo II) | piazza venezia 11

above left, above right, below left, below right: rome, viale america 229 | via labicana 144 | via del poggio laurentino 2 | via pinciana 35

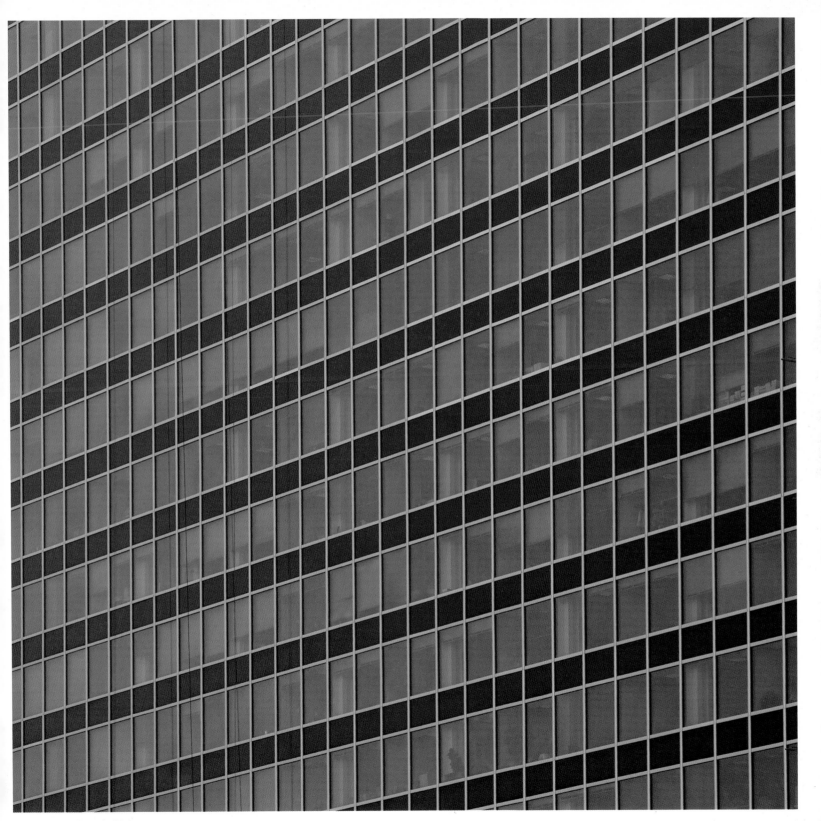

rome, viale dell' arte

rome, piazza del colosseo (colosseo)

stockholm

stockholm, stortorget 16

gustav-adolfs-torg 16 | tegnérgatan 8 (svenska missionskyrkan)

above left, below left, right: stockholm, strandvägen | kungsgatan | centralbron

stockholm, strandvägen

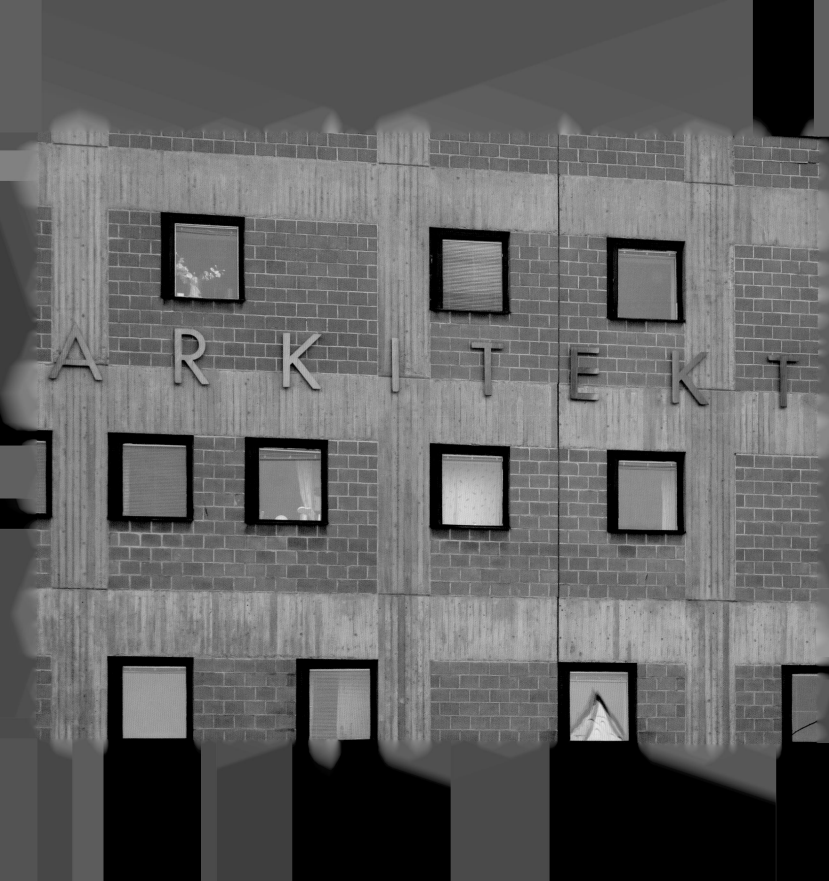

(gamla riksarkivet) | mäster samuelsgatan 42

st. petersburg

st. petersburg, dvortsovaia naberezhnaia 34 (zimnyi dvorets)

st. petersburg, ul. warschavskaja 23

vladimirski prospekt 19 | ulitsa warschavskaja 22 | vladimirski prospekt 2

vienna

vienna, aristide-de-sousa-mendes-promenade

above left, above right, below left, below right: vienna, taborstraße 1-3 | uraniastraße 1 | guglgasse 13 | marxergasse 1b

vienna, wagramer straße 3-5 (uno-city)

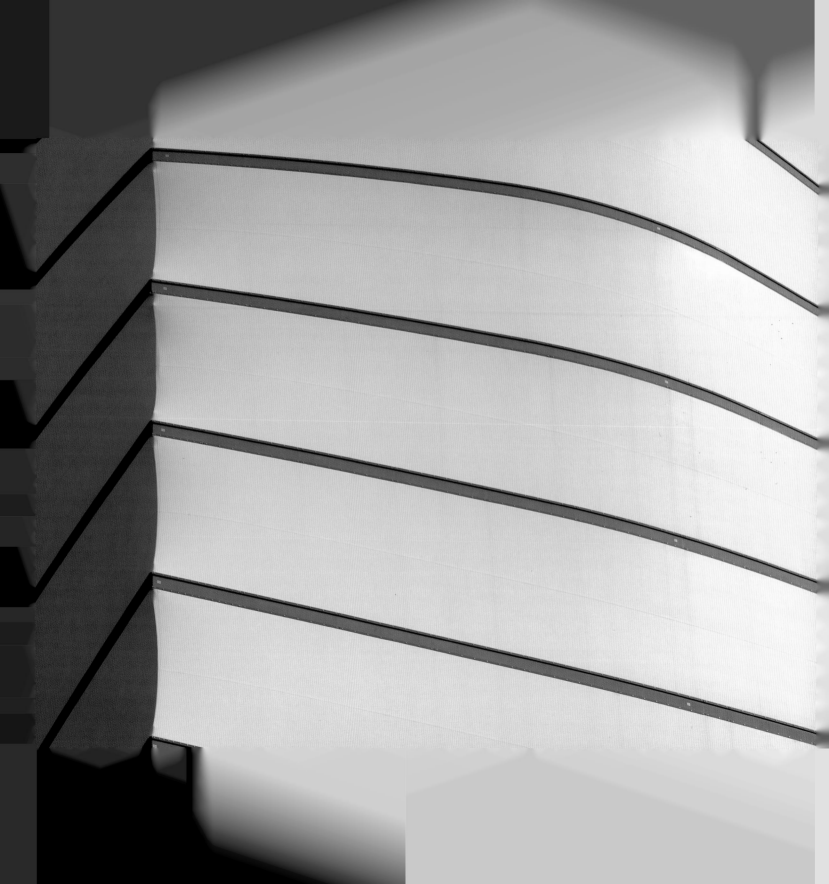

prater

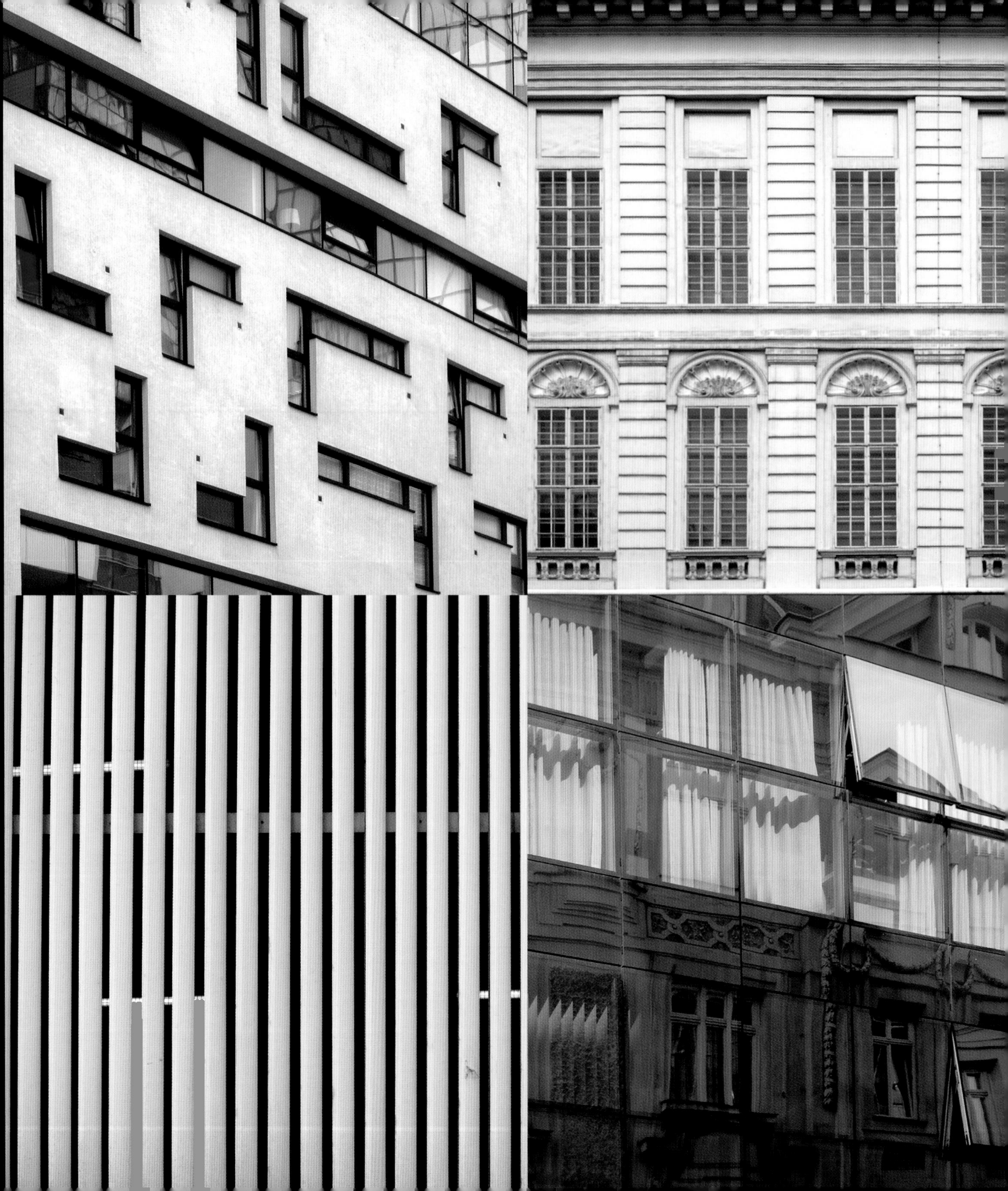

straße 4 | vordere zollamtstorstraße 13 | herrengasse 11

vilnius, aušros tor

above, below: vilnius, aušros vartų 6 (hotel europa royale) | ausros vartų 6 (hotel europa royale)

above left, above right, below left, below right: vilnius, 1. stuokos-gucevičiaus gatvė 3 (city park hotel) |
dominikonų gatvė 2 | jono basanavičiaus gatvė 4a | totorių gatvė 29

VITRAŽO MANUFAKTŪRA

vilnius, stiklių gatvė 6

vilnius, jono basanavičiaus gatvė 27

zurich

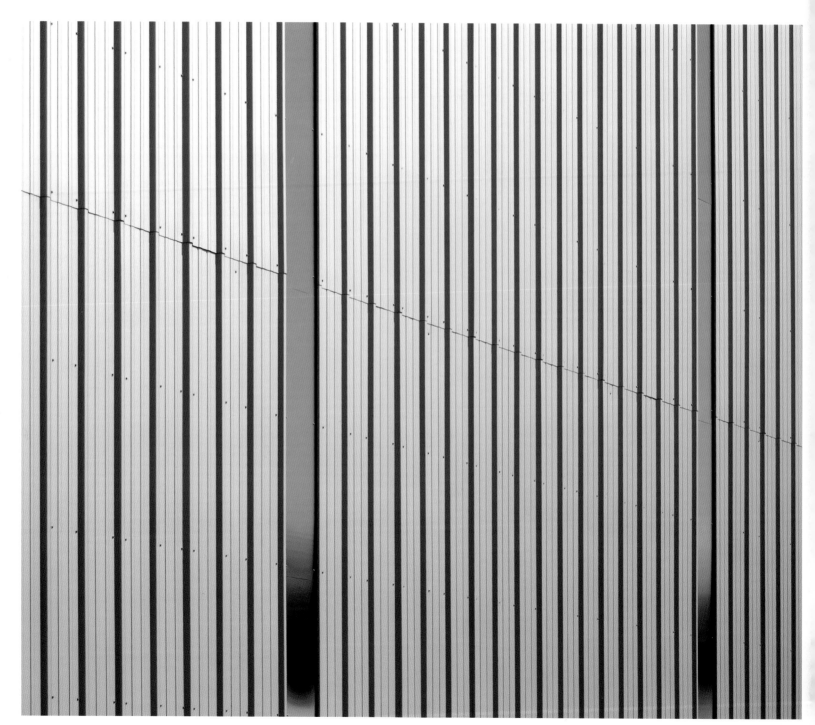

zurich, airport zurich-kloten

SADEURS

above left, above right, below left, below right: zurich, heimplatz 1 (kunsthaus)· | tannenstrasse 3 |
airport zurich-kloten | airport zurich-kloten

zurich, schiffbauerstrasse 11

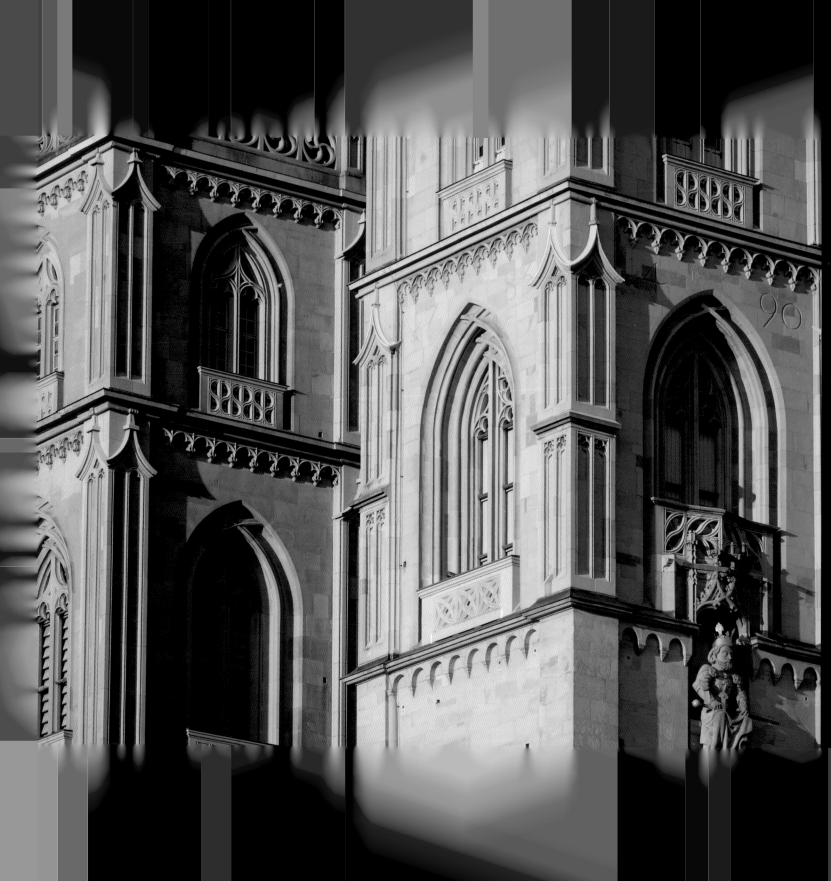

(universität zürich) | zollikerstrasse 141 | hardturmstrasse 11

photographers index

dominik butzmann   helsinki
www.dbutzmann.de

"what a dream – to wander the streets without a map, without
a schedule and collect impressions, colors, faces, light and
shadow!"

marius flucht   amsterdam, berlin
www.herrflucht.de

"look!"

katja hoffmann   ljubljana, london, vilnius
www.katjahoffmann.de

"without my camera I would have given up wanting to
understand the world."

jörn hustedt   copenhagen
www.hustedtnetwork.de

"photography for me is holding still of everything
subject to constant change."

thomas kierok   barcelona, vienna, zurich
www.kierok.de

"seeing is the way to awareness."

johannes kramer   athens, budapest, prague
johannes.kramer@berlin.de

**"photography for me is a confrontation with reality –
an interplay between objectivity and fantasy."**

marion lammersen   paris
www.marionlammersen.com

**"symbiosis of art and nature creates authentic and interesting
architecture."**

bernhardt link   istanbul, rome
www.link-foto.de

**"photographs reveal their own reality, or that, what the
photographer considers as such."**

kai senf   brussels
www.kaisenf.com

**"the organization and engineering of any architecture I perceive
in my viewfinder suggests a feeling of order that contrasts
the storm that is going on in my head. architecture photography
has a very meditative and calming effect on me."**

claudia schülke   st. petersburg
www.cs-fotodesign.com

**"to photograph something you need time.
if you don't have time, you can make snapshots."**

claudia weidemann   berlin, lisbon, riga, stockholm
c.weidemann@berlin.de

"photography changes my perception of reality."

katja zimmermann   cracow
office@beta-75.com

**"architecture itself carries stories out of the
centuries past behind the façades – photographs of
architecture tell us completely new stories."**